Extreme
PARKOUR

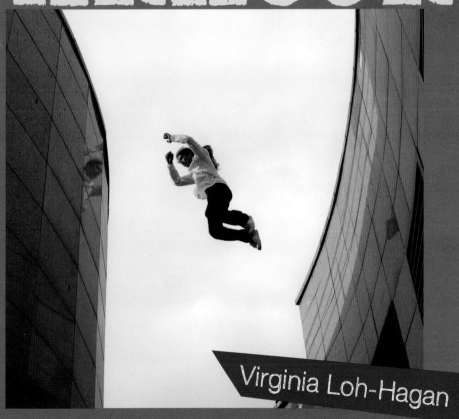

Virginia Loh-Hagan

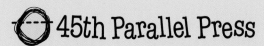
45th Parallel Press

Published in the United States of America by Cherry Lake Publishing
Ann Arbor, Michigan
www.cherrylakepublishing.com

Content Adviser: Liv Williams, Editor, www.iLivExtreme.com
Reading Adviser: Marla Conn, ReadAbility, Inc.
Photo Credits: ©Radin Myroslav/Shutterstock.com, cover, 1; ©Johnnyhetfield/istockphoto.com, 5; ©Alex Emanuel Koch/
Shutterstock.com, 6; ©Jacob Lund/Shutterstock.com, 8; ©Goruppa/istockphoto.com, 11; ©Hosam Salem/NurPhoto/
REX/Newscom, 12; ©Rommel Canlas/Shutterstock.com, 15; © BalicDalibor/istockphoto.com, 17; ©Matt Henry Gunther/
Thinkstock.com, 19; ©Cylonphoto/Dreamstime.com, 21; ©Samo Vidic/Red Bull Content Pool, 22; ©Jeremy Deputat/Red Bull
Content Pool, 25; ©Isantilli/Thinkstock.com, 27; ©Mikobagus/Dreamstime.com, 29; ©Trusjom/Shutterstock.com, multiple
interior pages; ©Kues/Shutterstock.com, multiple interior pages

45th Parallel Press is an imprint of Cherry Lake Publishing.

Library of Congress Cataloging-in-Publication Data

CIP data has been filed and is available at catalog.loc.gov

ABOUT THE AUTHOR

Dr. Virginia Loh-Hagan is an author, university professor, former classroom teacher, and
curriculum designer. She only runs if something is chasing her. She lives in San Diego
with her very tall husband and very naughty dogs. To learn more about her, visit
www.virginialoh.com.

Table of Contents

Parkour or Bust!

Who is Ryan Doyle? What's a traceur? What are obstacles? How is James Rudge unstoppable? Who is Shirley Darlington?

Ryan Doyle travels the world. In Greece, he jumped across rooftops. An animal was in his way. He **somersaulted**, or flipped, over it. He didn't stop moving. He kept running. In Turkey, he rolled down hills. He did backflips. In a river in Switzerland, he jumped from **boulder** to boulder. Boulders are large rocks. He skipped over the white waters. The world is Doyle's playground.

Doyle combines running and martial arts. He's a **traceur**. A traceur is someone who practices **parkour**. Traceurs overcome **obstacles**. Obstacles are objects in people's paths. They do it as fast as possible. They only use their bodies.

Doyle has poor eyesight. He's short. He almost lost his leg in a competition. He jumped from 12 feet (3.6 meters). He tried to do a flip. He missed the landing. His shinbone

Obstacles can be natural or man-made.

Traceurs overcome personal and environmental challenges.

snapped. His foot hung off his leg! Doctors removed his kneecap. They hammered bars and screws into his leg.

This didn't stop him. Doyle said, "I'm living proof that if you want it enough, you can get back on your feet. I'm so passionate about what I do that no matter what injury, I am just going to dust myself off and try again." He recovered. He returned to parkour.

James Rudge is also unstoppable. He was born with one arm. He somersaults off walls. Rudge started parkour at 12

Spotlight Biography: Anan Anwar

Anan Anwar went from teen pop star to parkour hero. He flips. He twists. He runs through temple ruins. He jumps across rooftops. He jumps down gaps between buildings. He is known for his creativity. Anwar was born in Thailand. His mother is Scottish. His father is Indonesian. He's a founding member of Team Farang. Team Farang is a Thai parkour crew. Farang means "foreigner" or "outsider." Anwar wants to see the world with fresh eyes. The group's goal is to bring parkour fans together. Friends come from all over the world. They travel together. They create together. Anwar gets ideas from talking to people. Once, he hosted 16 traceurs in his small apartment. He's focused on training and having fun.

Many traceurs are always climbing things.

years old. He said, "I have only ever known my body in this way. So, for me there isn't anything I can't do … it just means I have to try and be stronger in my right arm."

Parkour is not just for boys. Shirley Darlington is a founding member of Parkour Generations. That's a professional parkour group. She struggled to do a "muscle-up." This is a parkour move. She pulls up until she's waist high on a bar. Then she jumps to the top. She worked on this for several years. Today, Darlington parkours better than most men.

"Shirley Darlington is a founding member of Parkour Generations."

Body and Mind

What do traceurs do? Why do traceurs need strong bodies and minds?

Traceurs want to go from one place to another. They do it quickly. They do it with style. They imagine being chased. They want to get away as fast as possible. They run into obstacles. They don't waste movements. So, they don't go around obstacles. They learn to go over them.

There are no official moves in parkour. Traceurs run, jump, swing, roll, and climb. They decide which movements to use. They consider their surroundings. If they see a wall, they run toward it. They jump and push off the wall. They reach the top of the wall. If they see a gap, they jump. They catch ledges with their hands.

Traceurs are always looking for new paths. They **navigate**, or find, their way. They want to be creative. They want to be fast. Parkour can be done anywhere. But it's mostly an **urban** sport. That means in cities. Cities offer a lot of obstacles.

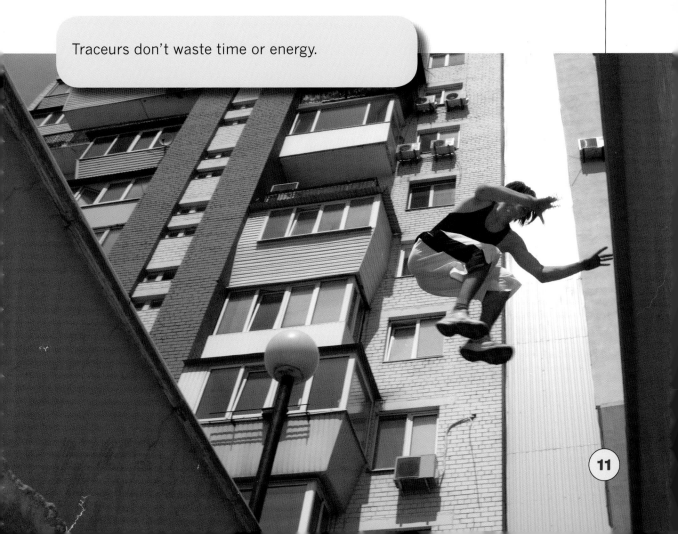

Traceurs don't waste time or energy.

Traceurs can parkour alone or in groups.

Parkour is also known as outdoor gymnastics or street tumbling. It is similar to freerunning. But freerunners perform more tricks and flips. They are focused on freedom of movement. Traceurs focus on getting from one place to another. They only perform tricks if doing so saves time. Parkour is not about showing off. It's about being smart.

Traceurs have strong bodies. They boost themselves over obstacles. They are only allowed to use their bodies.

When Extreme Is Too Extreme!

Alexander Rusinov is a Russian gymnast and traceur. He's also a daredevil. He does dangerous stunts. He's been called the Russian Spiderman. He started at a local playground. Then he moved on to his city's structures. He created his own style of handstand gymnastics. He climbs high walls. He jumps between rooftops. He does handstands on the edges of skyscrapers and bridges. He hangs from tall buildings. One of his most extreme stunts is dangling off construction equipment. He is giving the thumbs-up signal with the other hand. He dangles from hundreds of feet in the air. He doesn't use safety wires. He searches his city for high locations. He said, "I carefully plan for each new stunt I try and will never do something I know I'm not ready for. Through my training and preparations, I know I'll stay safe."

They maintain as much motion as possible.

Traceurs have strong minds. They think on their feet. They find paths quickly. They see their environment in a new way. They navigate it. They move around, across, through, over, and under obstacles.

They control their minds and bodies. Doyle describes parkour as an "art." It's about training. It about practicing.

"They see the environment in a new way."

Parkour requires strength and balance.

From French and Military Origins

How did parkour develop? Who is David Belle? What is Yamakasi? What are parkour's military roots? How did Georges Hebert inspire parkour?

Parkour was developed in France. It was developed in the 1980s. But Parkour has military roots. Georges Hebert was a French naval officer in World War I. He believed soldiers should be athletes and warriors. Hebert became a physical education trainer. He promoted obstacle courses. Soldiers performed all types of movements.

Raymond Belle trained using Hebert's methods. He was in the French Military. He became a heroic firefighter. His training influenced his son, David Belle.

David is a founder of parkour. He learned about military training from his father. He combined this with gymnastics and martial arts. He started the original parkour group with Sébastien Foucan. It's called Yamakasi. Yamakasi is a word from Congo. Congo is an African country. The word means being strong in body and spirit.

Parkour groups create a training method for overcoming physical and mental challenges.

Extreme Parkour: Know the Lingo

Breaking jumps: mastering a movement that's never been done before

Cat jump: jumping and landing with hands and feet on the obstacle

Demi-tour: making a U-turn

Equilibre: any type of balancing

Flow: performing moves smoothly and without pause

Gap jump: jumping over a gap between two objects

Parkour roll: rolling the shoulder across the ground and ending at the opposite hip

Precision jump: jumping and landing on a precise surface like a rail or wall ledge

Tic tac: pushing off an object and using a foot to gain height and reverse momentum in order to overcome another obstacle

Tricking: any sort of acrobatic stunt that combines martial arts, gymnastics, and/or break dancing

Underbar: jumping feet-first through an opening and grabbing a bar at the top to go through

Vault: any jump that uses the arms to overcome the obstacle

Wall run: running along the top of a wall

Parkour copied military obstacle training courses. Traceurs use cities and nature as obstacles.

Joining the group is hard. New people need support from a member. They need to pass tests. They need to value honesty, respect, and hard work. No excuses are allowed. No complaining is allowed.

Parkour and traceur are French words. Traceur comes from the French verb *tracer*. *Tracer* means "to draw a path." Parkour comes from the French phrase, *parcours du combatant*. It refers to Hebert's military obstacle training course.

Popularizing Parkour

How did parkour become popular? Who are Cory DeMeyers and Jesse La Flair? What is Tempest? What are some parkour competitions?

Parkour became popular in the late 1990s. David Belle's brother had pictures and videos of Yamakasi. He sent them to a French television show. Several television programs featured the videos.

More and more people became interested in parkour. Parkour was featured in some movies, **documentaries**, and advertisements. Documentaries are nonfiction films.

Online video sharing is the main reason why parkour is so popular. People all over the world know about parkour. Traceurs post and watch online videos of parkour. Videos show moves, experiments, and mistakes. Many people learn how to parkour from watching these videos.

Watching television shows inspired Cory DeMeyers. He watched the Teenage Mutant Ninja Turtles and Power

Parkour has become a global sport because of the media.

Corey DeMeyers was inspired by TV shows.

Rangers. He copied their flips. Then he saw a YouTube video of parkour. He said, "I want to do this with my life."

DeMeyers and Jesse La Flair use YouTube. They have a series on the Web. It's called *Off the Edge*. DeMeyers said, "It is crazy to think that parkour and freerunning are some of the most viewed videos on social media and have been for years, much more than any other sports."

That Happened?!?

Subway riders know to stay away from the tracks. Dylan Polin does not stay away. He posted a video of his parkour stunt at a Boston subway station. He flipped over subway tracks. He ran. Then, he stopped for a brief moment. Next, he hurled himself over the tracks. He jumped from platform to platform. He considered safety. He had friends on both sides. He waited for the train to come. He wrote, "Been dreaming of this for years. Finally gapped the Red Line train tracks." Polin has been practicing parkour for nearly 10 years. He said, "I spent the last few months getting mentally prepared for it ... I'm pretty happy about it." But officials are not happy. Officials called Polin's death-defying stunt "an incredibly foolish and extraordinarily stupid act."

DeMeyers and La Flair are both members of Tempest. It's an American parkour group. Tempest opened one of the first U.S. parkour gyms. It's called Tempest Academy.

La Flair said, "We see in pictures. We're very visual people who grew up in a visual medium." He has several thousand followers. His YouTube channel is the most popular parkour channel in the world.

La Flair and DeMeyers created a documentary called *From Here to There*. They traveled the world. They shared their adventures.

They host the Tempest Pro Takeover. La Flair said, "We're trying to be professional athletes in a sport that's not a professional sport." They've won awards in competitions like the Red Bull Art of Motion, International Parkour Competition, and North American Parkour Championship.

Some traceurs participate in competitions.

Concerns About Parkour

What do city officials worry about? What are the risks and dangers of parkour? How do traceurs stay safe?

Traceurs practice parkour in many different places. They practice in parks, streets, and buildings. City officials worry about traceurs damaging property. They worry about traceurs **trespassing**. Trespassing is entering a place without permission. City officials have **banned** parkour in some areas. Banned means to not allow.

Justin Casquejo practices parkour. He was arrested for trespassing. He sneaked in through a gap in a fence. He got past a security guard. He climbed up. He launched over obstacles such as ladders and stairs. He climbed to the top of the World Trade Center's tower. It is 1,775 feet (541 m) high. It's the highest building in the United States. His stunt was dangerous.

Common injuries are damaged joints and sprained ankles. Landing wrong causes many injuries.

Traceurs have to be careful of not breaking any laws.

Advice from the Field: Mandy Lam

Mandy Lam is a parkour athlete and instructor. She works at The Monkey Vault. It's a large movement training center. It's in Canada. Lam has been doing parkour for more than nine years. First, she studied martial arts. For her, parkour is about exploring movement. It's also about being outside. Lam admits that parkour is a male-dominated sport. She wants more women to try parkour. She advises, "With parkour, you're always starting at wherever you are at your own level. It's not meant to be a competitive sport. It's about exploring your own path. ... Use parkour to climb and find things you wouldn't usually see, and see things from a different perspective." Lam wants people to be more active. She wants people to use their bodies. She wants people to interact with objects.

Parkour can be dangerous. City officials worry about traceurs jumping off high buildings. There are many risks. They want traceurs to stay off rooftops.

There have been deaths. A Greek teenager fell though a glass skylight. He died. He was jumping between rooftops. He was trying to parkour. A Russian woman fell 17 stories. She died. She was on a rooftop. She ran. She jumped. She missed.

Traceurs practice parkour for many years. They start at smaller heights. They start with fewer obstacles. They are prepared. They know how to have fun. They know how to be safe. Parkour is an art and a sport.

Traceurs use a rolling motion to help absorb large impacts. This prevents injuries.

Did You Know?

- *Tracers* is an action movie about parkour. It stars Taylor Lautner. His character joins a parkour group. He did extensive training in Los Angeles. His toughest stunt was a wall run. He ran from the ground up onto the wall.

- The film *Casino Royale* featured Sébastien Foucan in a chase scene. It takes place early in the movie.

- James Gallion has cerebral palsy. He does parkour to experience movement and a feeling of confidence.

- Jackie Chan is known as the unofficial father of parkour. Chan was doing parkour before it was parkour. He has starred in many action movies. He does his own dangerous stunts. He runs through streets while avoiding enemies, climbing walls and jumping over cars.

- Giulio Calisse scales buildings. He photographs traceurs performing stunts. He photographs them hanging on ledges. He's been shooting parkour photos for 10 years.

- David Belle showed a parkour video to Hubert Kounde. Kounde suggested changing the c in parcours to a k. The letter k seemed stronger. He also suggested removing the s.

- Jesse La Flair does stunts in *Teenage Mutant Ninja Turtles* and *Divergent*.

Consider This!

TAKE A POSITION! Parkour has no rules, teams, or points. Some feel parkour is a way of life. They feel it's more an art expression than a sport. Do you think it's a sport or not? Argue your point with reasons and evidence.

SAY WHAT? Parkour and freerunning are often considered to be the same thing. Explain the similarities and differences between parkour and freerunning.

THINK ABOUT IT! Some traceurs practice parkour in gyms. But many traceurs do not like this idea. They feel it goes against parkour values of creativity and freedom. They think parkour should be practiced outside in cities and nature. What do you think about this?

SEE A DIFFERENT SIDE! Mark Toorock is a traceur. He says injuries are rare. He said, "Participants rely not on what they can't control—wheels or the icy surfaces of snowboarding and skiing—but their own hands and feet." Imagine you're a city official and you're concerned about safety. What do you think of Toorock's statement?

Learn More: Resources

PRIMARY SOURCES

Foucan, Sébastien. *Free Running: The Urban Landscape Is Your Playground*. Berkeley, CA: Ulysses Press, 2009.

From Here to There, a documentary (2014).

SECONDARY SOURCES

Edwardes, Dan. *The Parkour and Freerunning Handbook*. New York: Dey Street Books, 2009.

WEB SITES

American Parkour: http://americanparkour.com

World Freerunning Parkour Federation: www.wfpf.com

Glossary

banned (BAND) not allowed

boulder (BOHL-dur) a large rock

documentaries (dahk-yuh-MEN-tur-eez) films about real people and real events

navigate (NAV-ih-gate) to find one's way

obstacles (AHB-stuh-kuhlz) objects, natural or man-made

parkour (par-KOOR) a sport that combines running, gymnastics, martial arts, and break dancing as a person goes from one place to another

somersaulted (SUHM-ur-sawlt-id) did an acrobatic move in which you turned head over heels

traceur (TRAY-sur) a person who practices parkour

trespassing (TRES-pas-eng) entering a place without permission

urban (UR-buhn) city

Index